Nathaniel Brassey Halhed

The Letters of Detector

on the Seventh and Eighth Reports of the Select Committee, and on the

India Regulating Bill

Nathaniel Brassey Halhed

The Letters of Detector
on the Seventh and Eighth Reports of the Select Committee, and on the India Regulating Bill

ISBN/EAN: 9783743687233

Printed in Europe, USA, Canada, Australia, Japan

Cover: Foto ©ninafisch / pixelio.de

More available books at **www.hansebooks.com**

THE
LETTERS
OF
DETECTOR,

ON THE

Seventh and Eighth

REPORTS

OF THE

SELECT COMMITTEE,

AND ON THE

INDIA REGULATING BILL.

LONDON:

Printed in the Year 1783.

On the SEVENTH REPORT of the SELECT COMMITTEE.

ON the eve of an Election for Directors to ferve the Eaft-India Company, and at a moment when the Proprietary have an urgent neceffity for exercifing the moft unbiaffed judgment, in chufing the future Guardians of their expiring privileges, appears a thundering Report from the Select Committee, arraigning the conduct of the late Chairman and Deputy, at prefent out by rotation, and Candidates for re-election. Recollecting, as I do, with all poffible veneration, the former very candid and public-fpirited ftrictures of this refpectable body, and fully awake to the difintereftednefs of their labours, I am exceedingly hurt that the obligation of feizing the earlieft opportunity to draw the attention of the Houfe of Commons to matters of fuch magnitude, fhould give envy and fcandal a plea (however groundlefs) for fuf-

B   pecting

pecting fomething of perfonality, or private
end, in the compofition and publication of
the prefent Report. It will be faid (and I
am forry that I have not now time to refute
the charge) that the crifis chofen for print-
ing this Report is, of itfelf, a convincing argument of the illiberality of its principles.
That while the blame (if any blame there
be) with refpect to the feveral tranfactions
there mentioned, will be found ultimately
to reft *in toto* with the Secretary to the
Committee of Secrecy at the India-Houfe,
the main efforts of the Report are aimed
againft the character of Mr. Sulivan.—That
as it is the very birth-right and unalienable
privilege of a Britifh fubject, to be heard in
his defence, and to be tried by his peers—
fo it is the greateft invafion of that privilege, and the moft tyrannous oppreffion of
that birth-right, to infinuate criminality before conviction; to prejudice the Jury by
anticipated fentence, and by a premature
trial to preclude the poffibility of exculpa-
tion.—It will therefore, I fear, be whifpered,
that it is an attempt to miflead the judgment
of the Proprietors, and to hurt Mr. Sulivan
in his election.---And as no man, who fhall
come calmly to the perufal of the Report,
can poffibly hefitate, for a moment, in pro-
nouncing that gentleman's innocence, I am
                                                    much

much alarmed, left national spirit and honest indignation should so far get the better of private engagements, or personal dislike, or prudential caution, in the present instance, as to insure Mr. Sulivan's election, with a majority equal to that by which Mr. Hastings very lately triumphed over a no less equitable manœuvre.

Shame to be cajoled by what may be represented as so flimsy an artifice, conscious abhorrence of imbibing prejudices from *ex Parte* evidence, and real sympathy for the common danger of having all our individual rights and characters thus wantonly, thus interestedly, and thus injuriously torn to pieces, will operate most effectually to the counteraction of that system, which many may suspect the Report to have been calculated to promote : *and as the mind naturally loves to fix on persons rather than things,* it is to be apprehended, that, if an idea of any unfairness or lurking treachery in the compilation of this Report, should once unfortunately make its way,—the eyes of the public will naturally be turned on the acknowledged Compiler. This is the circumstance I most dread, —this is the point which all well-wishers to the Report should labour to obviate. Should this once obtain, motives and designs, and consequences respecting the critical moment

of

of promulgation and infidious management of the charge, will burſt forth into conviction. The Chairman of the Select Committee will then be well underſtood to pit himſelf againſt the reſpectable Candidate, who has been eight times Chairman at the India-Houſe : as another great reporter has caſt his gauntlet at the Governor General of Bengal. *Dii boni! homo homini quantum diſtat!*—The Honourable General has, however, ſecured himſelf one advantage in the preſent Conteſt, by being no longer in a capacity to infult the feelings of the Proprietary, or aggravate their abhorrence of his Character and Principles, by nauſeous declamations.

For myſelf, wiſhing moſt ſincerely well to the cauſe of truth and juſtice, I can but call on the Independent and diſintereſted Proprietors of India-Stock, to interpoſe effectually, for the preſervation of their own Freedom of Election; and to ſupport, againſt the machinations of intereſted malice, that character, for firmneſs and conſiſtency, which in two inſtances they have lately ſo honourably acquired, by defeating all the overtures of Miniſterial Corruption, and all the bluſterings of Unconſtitutional Authority.

Much as I reſpect the general principles on which this laſt and ſeventh Report from the

the Select Committee is founded, I shall take
the liberty of expressing my sentiments on
some of its articles, in which I am so unfortunate as not entirely to acquiesce.

In the first place, I beg leave to observe,
that the late act for regulating the Judicature
in Bengal, owes its existence to the Select
Committee. The sole effective product of
seven voluminous Reports, it was the dar-
ling of their labours, the plea at once and
pledge of their existence: and no wonder
that their vanity was gratified in contempla-
tion of its importance, and their passions interested in the completion of its objects.
Hence the eagerness with which they have
traced its progress to India, and the solici-
tude with which they watched its fate:
hence too we must account for their appa-
rently wilful ignorance of its arrival at Calcutta, in their undiscerning fury for its original miscarriage.

The public will, no doubt, consider the
Select Committee as perfectly justified, and
even laudably anxious in ascertaining to a
point of indisputable certainty, the dispatch
of this regulating act to India: and in being
somewhat warm at any delay, either casual
or designed. But it will probably conceive
them to have reason to be fully pacified, or
at least to abate part of their inveteracy,

on

on learning that the faid Act did really proceed to India by the firft difpatch of that
nature, by which Acts of Parliament were
ufually tranfmitted ; and was in no refpect
othérways retarded, than by the unavoidable accidents of a fea voyage ; and is known
to have been within a week's diftance from
Bengal upwards of nine months ago.

 With nothing more than a previous knowledge of this fact, how eafily may every
fyllable of criminatory matter againft Mr.
Sulivan, and Sir William James, as urged in
the Seventh Report, be done away! Let
but the reader anticipate each fentence of
the Report with recollection of this fingle
circumftance, and I leave the reft, with the
utmoft confidence, to his own confcience.—
We will now take a little furvey of the
whole tranfaction.

 In July, 1781, the Bengal Judicature Act
paffed in Parliament. In Auguft, the Tryal Sloop was difpatched with packets from
the India Company, to their feveral prefidencies, and copies of this Act were then fent
on board (Seventh Report, page 5). In December, 1781, the Select Committee examined Mr. Sulivan, then Chairman of the
Court of Directors, refpecting the difpatch
of the Judicature Act. His evidence was
full, complete, and (as I ftill think, with all
deference

deference to the Commitee) fully fatisfactory,
in regard to the tranfmiffion of the Acts by
the Tryal Sloop. But Mr. Sulivan, with
the care of the commerce and finance, the
politics and legiflation, all the internal and
external arrangements of all the Company's
affairs, abroad and at home, on his fhoulders,
had forgotten to fend by an early opportunity an order for the retribution of certain individuals in India, for acts of oppreffion committed on them by the Supreme Court, to
which he ftood pledged, as Chairman of
the Company. It was an overfight, not
poffible to be accounted for but by the hur-
ry of bufinefs. Neither Mr. Sulivan nor
his friends, nor his remoteft connections
could lofe or gain a fhilling by this retribution. It would neither have committed
his authority, nor affected his interefts. He
acknowledged the omiffion, fubmitted to the
cenfure, and rectified the error by the very
firft occafion. But on the fubject of tranfmitting the Act itfelf, he urged that it had
been fent by the Tryal Sloop, the very firft
public conveyance, within a month of its
being in print; that no other means of difpatch had offered, and that the packet had
been unfortunately retarded by ftrefs of
weather.

The Tryal floop finally failed in February,
1782,

1782, and by various letters now in England, it is well known that she parted from Ganjam (less than a week's sail from Bengal) on the 3d of July last, carrying with her both the Act in question, and the orders for indemnification of the Patna Magistrates. Mr. Sulivan's evidence therefore has been, from first to last, uniform, undesigning, and strictly to the point. He originally deposed, that the Acts went in the Tryal Sloop, and that it was sent with the Company's only public dispatch. It has been proved in the first Report (page 11), that a General Letter from the Court of Directors, is the usual and official channel for communicating Acts of Parliament to their servants abroad ; and it is now certain, that the said Judicature Acts arrived in India, in the Tryal Sloop, in July last.

The Select Committee then examined Mr. Wilkes, Secretary to the Secret Committee, at the India-House, to discover whether any secret dispatches had been sent from the India-House, in the interval, between the first publication of the Judicature Act, and its final dispatch in the Tryal Sloop. From him they learnt that a packet had been sent away by sea on the 3d of August, the very day after the Act in question was printed, and what seems to have surprised them much,

much, that copies of the faid Act were inclofed in that packet.

Here was opened a glorious fcene for malicious conjecture, and perplexing crofs-
queftions. The Chairman had acknowledged nothing but a public conveyance by
the Tryal Sloop—the Secretary hinted, in
myfterious terms, a private difpatch.

In whatever confufion this matter might
have been involved, at the time of Mr.
Wilkes's firft examination, it is now known,
that thefe difpatches of the 3d of Auguft,
were fent on board two Men of War, under
fecret failing orders, but deftined for India :
and that in confequence of fome other ne-
ceffities of the State, the faid fhips did not
perform their route to India, but returned
to England in October, and the Difpatches
from the Company were fent back to the
India-Houfe early in the month of November.—Mr. Sulivan, therefore, who gave
his evidence to the Select Committee in
December, and who had never confidered
the Difpatch of the 3d of Auguft but as of
a private nature, and within the ftricteft
conftruction of a *State Secret*, might naturally, and with propriety, deem it *equivalent
to no difpatch at all*; and therefore, fo far
from leading the Committee into an error
on that head (page 14), he gave them no

C   grounds

grounds for fufpicion of the poffibility of fuch a circumftance. But the embarraffment and perplexity of the Secretary, on his in-quifitorial examination, having given the Select Committee much room for unfair ani-madverfion, it was permitted him to trench fo far upon this Secret, as to acknowledge the Difpatch of the 3d of Auguft.

To this fingle circumftance may, I think, be afcribed the very exiftence of the Seventh Report, and I defy the acuteft of mankind to difcover the truth of the tranfaction, or to unravel the confufion of cenfure, as in-volved in the purpofed obfcurity of that Re-port, without fome collateral knowledge or information. And this I fhall now en-deavour to fupply.—

Appendix, No. 2, A, of the Seventh Re-port, contains the original draft of a letter from the Committee of Secrecy at the India-Houfe, to Bengal, dated the 1ft of Auguft, 1781, and fent on the 3d of the fame month on board the Men of War, as above mentioned.

This letter is incontrovertibly proved to have contained no mention whatever of the Judicature Act; for the words, " *Act paffed*," which are now, by implication, underftood to fignify the Judicature Act, have been foifted in, fince the letter returned from the King's

King's ſhips, in the place of the real word, " *Appendixes,*" and the ſentence, in its firſt ſtate, ran thus, "We now ſend another " Copy of that Report, and of the *Appen-* " *dixes,* for your further information." This paragraph is clearly in the official language of communication. But when the word *Appendixes* was altered to *Act paſſed,* and the ſentence made to run in this manner, " We now ſend another Copy of that Re- " port, and of the *Act paſſed,* for your further " information," the ſenſe itſelf is muti- lated, the connexion broken, and the fiction evident. For who would think of ſending an Act of Parliament by way of information? And who would uſe the indefinite terms, of an *Act paſſed,* as deſcriptive of a particular Act on a particular ſubject? This is not the ſtyle of buſineſs:—and common ſenſe would have combined with official experience in the Chairman or Deputy to correct the paſſage, had it ever been ſhewn or recited to either of them. But Mr. Wilkes's own evidence proves that it was done totally without their previous advice, and that "*There were no* " *orders given for it"* (page 9), nor did he ever *ſhew Mr. Sulivan the papers after the* *alteration was made* (page 12).

On the return of that Diſpatch, and about the time of Mr. Sulivan's Examination,

Mr.

Mr. Wilkes called upon Mr. Sulivan, and told him the Judicature Act had been sent in it,—(see his Evidence, 7th Report, page 11) he says, " I called upon Mr. Sulivan, and " told him the Judicature Acts had been sent: " he knew the Packets were come back : " he directed me to bring the Letter, which " I did, before there was any alteration made " in it. He said, he observed there was no. " mention made of the Judicature Act in " the Letter. This is the substance of what " passed between us."—Mr. Wilkes made up the Packet,—not Mr. Sulivan,—Mr. Wilkes asserted that the Judicature Act had been inclosed in it,—Mr. Sulivan opposed to this, the omission of all mention of it in the Letter. Mr. Wilkes persisted in his first assertion, and, without any instruction from Mr. Sulivan, went home and altered the Letter, which he never shewed to Mr. Sulivan afterwards.

The Select Committee, in the 6th page of the Report, have the following paragraph :

" Your Committee having perused these " papers (i. e. the draft of letter of the 3d " of August) must remark to the House the " very different manner in which the Com— " mittee of Secrecy *mentioned the two Acts.* " The Judicature Act, which, amongst " other important points, gave relief to the. " Patna

" Patna Magiftrates, is fent for the infor-
" mation of the Council General, without any
" injunction of obedience or attention to it:
" But in the very next fentence, when the
" Act of the prolongation of the Charter is
" mentioned, then it is faid to be fent, not
" for their information only, but for their
" guidance alfo, and ftrict attention and
" obedience is enjoined thereto."

So palpable an infult on common fenfe
and common juftice, I did not think compatible even with Afiatic depravity of foul.
The character of an innocent man is firft of
all deliberately impeached by groundlefs
infinuation; and it is then proved beyond
the poffibility of cavil (pages 11 and 12), and
afterwards in the very words of the Report
(page 14), that, " not only from his own"
(Mr. Wilkes's) " confeffion, but from the
" alteration in the Records, it evidently ap-
" pears, that no mention whatfoever had
" been made in the letter of the 3d of Au-
" guft, 1781, of the tranfmiffion of the Ju-
" dicature Act."

Can any terms be too grofs for fo infa-
mous a violation of every thing juft, and
manly, and decent? The Reporter firft takes
up the falfe fide of the queftion, and from
thence, by a jefuitical and unfair inference,
draws a criminatory charge againft the
Chairman

Chairman of the Company, whom he knew
at the time to be unconcerned in the whole
tranfaction ; and, in a very few pages afterwards, thunders againft the embarraffed Secretary as author of that very falfification,
from which he had but the inftant before
taken advantage to deduce a moft calumni-
ous and unwarrantable conclufion.

If thefe be the weapons by which he
means to affail Mr. Sulivan and Sir Wm.
James, I affure him they will all rebound back
upon himfelf, without any prejudice to his
antagonifts ; and I would advife him to
adopt the more effectual, and lefs diabolical
inftruments of poifon or affaffination, to ac-
complifh his purpofe.

After all, the remark is no lefs ridiculous
than bafe ; for what is the difference between tranfmitting one Act of Parliament
for information, and another for obedience :—
They were both to be tranfmitted to the fubjects of the fame State, and would become
obligatory without any notice or injunction
whatfoever from the Chairman and his Deputy ; for in what method could they incul-
cate obedience to thofe who fhould be in-
clined to difobey an Act of Parliament ? and
how could they fuppofe *their* orders likely
to be more effectual than the laws of their
country ? And even admitting all this heap

of

of abfurdity, it makes nothing againſt the paragraph in queſtion; for the operation of the Judicature Act extended only to the Members of the Supreme Court, and to them moſt certainly the authority of the Chairman and his Deputy did not reach. So that even in this ſtate of the fact they *might* have ſent the Act for their information, but could not poffibly give them *orders* to obey it. The Honourable General, I find by this and other inſtances of falſe logic, is not an adept in the Ariſtotelian Science : His *doctors* have not been of the claſs of *irrefragables.*

Mr. Sulivan the Chairman, or Sir Wm. James his Deputy, or both, are next criminated for having (as it is infiſted page 15) " given permiffion to the fictitious paragraph " of the letter of the 3d of Auguſt being " preſented to your Committee as the real " paragraph of the letter of the Committee " of Secrecy of that date."

Upon this article it is only given in evidence, page 14, " that when orders are ſent " from a Committee of the Houſe of Com- " mons, for any papers, or copies of papers, " that the proper officer waits upon the " Chairman or Deputy Chairman of the " Eaſt-India Company, to receive inſtruc- " tions, and that the orders ſo received from " a Com-

" a Committee of this Houfe are read and
" minuted by the Court of Directors at their
" next meeting." To what, therefore, does
this teftimony amount? To nothing more,
than that the Secretary muft have waited on
the Chairman or Deputy for inftructions:
that his inftructions muft have been, that
he fhould furnifh the Select Committee with
the letter in demand, and that he carried
that letter in which he had previoufly in-
ferted his own authorized alterations.

Not a particle of proof here, or even of
implication, to lead to a belief that either the
Chairman or his Deputy faw the letter before its tranfmiffion to the Select Committee,
much lefs that they authorized the prefentation of the fictitious paragraph. And, indeed, Mr. Wilkes exprefsly affirms, (page
12,) that " *he did not fhew the Papers, after*
" *the alterations, to Mr. Sulivan.*"—Here,
then we have another infinuation, equally
well founded with the former, and no lefs
characteriftic of the principles and views of
its inventive parent.

I have pretty well got over the *principal*
articles of Accufation, and, I hope, fully
refuted them. Of the *fmaller* animadver-
fions, one is, the omiffion to fend the Judicature Act, by Meffieurs Dunkin and Smart,
who commenced their journey to India, by
land,

land, on the 8th of December, 1781. To this objection it may be anfwered, that the Packets fent by land from the Committee of Secrecy, are always very concife, and moft commonly in cypher; that it was totally unufual to fend an Act of Parliament by any other than a Sea conveyance, and inclofed in a General Letter (1ft Report, pages 11 and 32); and that there was good reafon to hope, that the Tryal Sloop might get to India as early as the land Difpatch. Events have fully juftified the expectation; for Meffieurs Dunkin and Smart, arrived at Bombay on the 20th of May, and are known to have been at Madras in the middle of July. The Tryal Sloop arrived at Ganjam (upwards of 400 miles beyond Madras) on the 2d of July, and failed for Bengal on the 3d, where fhe muft have arrived by the 8th at fartheft.

A few words on the ftory of the Box, related in pages 12 and 13 of the Report. The box itfelf, the marks, &c. are all plaufibly accounted for; the only doubt is about the feal. It is proved that Mr. Stephens, of the Admiralty, received and returned a *fealed* Packet. Mr. Owen's evidence *leads to a fufpicion*, that the Packet, of which he was called to teftify the contents, was *not fealed*. This concerns Mr. Wilkes *alone*, and an Affidavit from Mr. Owen or Mr. Wilkes,

D   muft

muſt here be the only method for coming at the truth *: and let it turn out as it may, Mr. Sulivan and Sir William James have nothing to do with it.

In the firſt page of the Report, the " Com-
" mittee beg leave to inform the Houſe, that
" twenty months being elapſed ſince the
" Judicature Act was paſſed, and *no advice*
" *of its promulgation* being arrived, altho'
" evidence had been given of its being
" ſent on the 3d. of Auguſt, 1781, your
" Committee thought it highly neceſſary to
" examine into all the circumſtances of the
" tranſmiſſion of that Act, by the Diſpatch
" of the 3d of Auguſt."

The reſult of that examination has been already diſcuſſed, and the whole jumble of inconſiſtent Charges huddled together in the Report, upon this original Error in Mr. Wilkes's evidence, I have above explained and done away. At preſent, I only mean to recall the attention of the Public to the aſſertion, that *no advice of the promul-gation of the Act in India has yet arriv-ed.* The Report, indeed, is very careful that this circumſtance ſhall not be overlook-ed; for we find it again induſtriouſly thruſt

---

* Mr. Wilkes has ſince cleared up the matter by a circumſtantial affidavit.

forward

forward in page 17th and laft, " finally, that " although it is now upwards of 20 months " fince the Act was paffed, no account of " its being arrived at Bengal has yet been " received by the India Company.".

Thefe two attempts, to convey a totally falfe idea in words compatible with meer truth, are of fo fhallow and flimfy a texture, that I fufpect the compiler of the Report to have concealed their infertion from all his more difcerning or fcrupulous Colleagues.

It is indifputably true that there is no intelligence of the *promulgation* of the Judicature Act in India, and equally fo, that the India Company (*in its collective capacity*), has received no (*official*) account of its arrival in India. But that the Tryal Sloop arrived at Ganjam on the 2d of July, 1782, and failed from thence on the 3d for Calcutta, is as well known to every individual connected with the Company, as the exiftence of the Judicature Act itfelf; and in July the paffage from Ganjam to Calcutta is as fafe by water as the Ferry over the Thames at Weftminfter Bridge. So that a week beyond the 2d of July is much more than ample allowance for its actual promulgation at Calcutta.

This Seventh Report therefore is founded

upon

upon the fame minute attention to the ftate of facts, upon the fame liberality of fentiment, and patriotic confiderations for public utility, as the Six preceding excellent compofitions, on which I have already had the honour to offer a few remarks. It is an admirable addition to the original work, and compleats the honourable compiler's digeft of fabricated criminality. In the laft Seffions the Honourable General was pleafed to pronounce an elaborate panegyric on the extraordinary merits of his Honourable Friend's Six Reports: The illuftrious Author has lately returned the adulatory incenfe in an extravagant compliment on the prefent mafter-piece of the General. As the merits of both are nearly equal, fo I think are their chances for the affent and approbation of the Public.

Qui Bavium non odit, amet tua Carmina,
Mævi.

D E T E C T O R.
7th April, 1783.

On the new BILL, *propoſed for the better*
REGULATION *of the* BRITISH POSSES-
SIONS *in* INDIA:

LETTER I.

Mr. EDITOR,

THE Secret Committee of the Houſe
of Commons, appointed to inveſti-
gate the cauſes of the war in the Carnatic,
acquired, in the courſe of their labours, ſuch
an extenſive knowledge of all the Eaſt-India Company's concerns, as to be competent for new-modelling every branch of Government, and overturning every principle of
policy in all our Aſiatic poſſeſſions. Their
enquiries with reſpect to this war ſeemed to
be cloſed laſt ſeſſions in 44 reſolutions, of
which (although *paſſed* by a very thin meeting of the Houſe of Commons) it is fair to
ſay, that they were received with little credit or reſpect by the nation at large : that
they were minutely, though candidly, can-
vaſſed, and in great part ſatisfactorily refuted.
Whatever might be the motive that produced theſe haſty reſolutions, their effect has
indeed been very inconſiderable. The war
in the Carnatic ſtill rages, and the cauſe of
its commencement is ſtill as obſcure as the
period

period of its termination. Political empiri-
cifm has hitherto prefcribed no effectual remedy for the diforder, nor has Hyder Ally
fhewn the flighteft tendency to pacification
in return for our voluntary effufions of moderation and forbearance. If, however, an
idea of parliamentary interpofition hath already fo far operated on the Councils of the
Mahrattas, as to caufe delay in the ratifica-
tion of that treaty to which they had previoufly, by their plenipotentiary, given a full
affent; if a reliance on the diftractions of
our government and the mutability of our
fyftems hath infpired our enemies with frefh
courage for the profecution of hoftilities
abroad: *here*, at leaft, our Committees have
effectually anfwered the purpofes of their
appointment. Delinquency has been clearly defined, accurately traced out, and incontrovertibly convicted. Bills of pains and pe-
nalties have been urged with unufual feve-
rity : and while affiftance for the vigorous
conduct of the war has been dealt out with
a parfimonious and fufpicious referve, all the
weapons of perfecution have been whetted
againft the devoted objects, to whofe inat-
tention or incapacity the origin of the ca-
lamity feems to have been imputed; juft as
if a furgeon, after performing amputation in
a dangerous fracture, fhould employ himfelf

felf in cutting and anatomizing the diftem-
pered limb, inftead of applying the bandages,
and fuppreffing the hæmorrhage. While the
Reports of the Secret Committee appeared
to bear uncommonly hard on certain Members of the Madras Government, while Hyder's invafion was *in them* reprefented as
the joint product of ambition and refent-
ment, men looked for the caufes of the
war to the feat of its ravages; and thought
that the mere deftination of hoftilities fufficiently difcriminated their motive. But
the Refolutions founded on thofe Reports
quickly opened their eyes, and attributed by a
chain of fanciful, remote, arbitrary deductions,
a portion of the misfortune to the Governor
General of Bengal. Slight, however, as his
fhare in the blame of this tranfaction muft
neceffarily have been, and vifionary as the
imputation will moft certainly appear to all
who fhall take the trouble to perufe the Reports, he was marked out as the firft object
of reprehenfion, and the Houfe of Commons was, by fome management, prevailed
upon to vote his recal.

We can all well recollect the different
manœuvres practifed at the eaft and weft ends
of the town, for effecting this laudable purpofe: and we feel an honeft exultation in
proclaiming, that the fpirited efforts of an
extra-

extraordinary majority in the Court of Proprietors baffled (as both by law and the
principles of their charter they were au-
thorifed to do) all thofe attempts. A fet of
men, deeply and perfonally interefted in the
profperity of Indian affairs, agreed, *fix to one,*
to entruft the management and prefervation
of their property to a man, whom a fudden
and unfatisfactory vote of an inconfiderable
part of one branch of the legiflature tended
to banifh from their fervice. About 40
members of the Houfe of Commons, carried
the refolution for Mr. Haftings's recal; upwards of 420 proprietors of India ftock,
united for his continuation. Leaving the
doctrine of parliamentary infallibility to thofe
who have never read reports or refolutions,
I fhall not fcruple to affirm, and to put it to
the confcience of every man of common
fenfe, that 420 refpectable proprietors of
India ftock, are collectively as able judges
of the merits and demerits of Mr. Haftings,
as any forty members who ever fat in the
Houfe. I will go farther, and will affert it
as my moft unalterable conviction, that the
number of Members of Parliament who bal-
lotted in their proprietary capacity for the
Governor General's continuation, far exceed-
ed thofe who in the Houfe were content

by

by a filent nod to authenticate the refolution
for his removal.

But, though the cloud of laft feffions
paffed over innocuous, the ftorm ftill con-
tinued to gather: and is now burft in the
tremendous thunder of a Bill ! If Mr. Haftings could heretofore ftem the ftream of
partiality in a vote of the Commons, he fhall
now be overwhelmed by a torrent of the
whole Legiflature. If the Proprietors of
India ftock wifely and confcientioufly con-
tributed to his continuation in their fervice
by a legal and conftitutional exertion of their
prerogative, that prerogative fhall therefore
be abolifhed by *law*. If the India Company
has been preferved at the very inftant of
bankruptcy, and if their foreign poffeffions
have been defended by exertions bordering
on impoffibility : if the whole train of their
affairs have been gradually improved from
confufion and diffipation, to fyftem, to
œconomy, to profperity, by the man of
their unbiaffed and deliberate choice, felected,
approved, and confirmed to the fame office
by three fucceffive Acts of Parliament at
diftinct and diftant periods ; thofe Acts
fhall now be abrogated in a moment ; that
man fhall be violently removed by a new
law, and the Company's right of nominating,
continuing, or difplacing, not only this, but

E   all

all their other confidential fervants in the
whole extent of their fettlements, fhall be for
ever done away! The only vifible plea or
pretence for this infringement of the charter, this invafion of property, this bare-
faced exertion of defpotifm, is the dif-
miffion of Governor General Haftings. To
remove him, nothing lefs than an Act of
Parliament could fuffice : and permiffion for
bringing in an Act to this purpofe, being
once obtained, every additional encroach-
ment on the Company's rights that could be
any how foifted in, was fo much clear gain
to the Courtly fyftem of arbitrary Patronage.
Every ufeful, every plaufible alteration propofed by the prefent bill is fully compatible with the Company's actual powers under their Charter ; and if the collective experience of a fet of men of bufinefs, who
have feen, as Directors of long ftanding,
the caufes of moft of our calamities in Afia,
and as Proprietors have felt their effects, be
not adequate to the difcovery of the proper
remedies, furely the occafional perufal of a
number of temporary records in the courfe
of the fittings of a Committee for two Seffions, and with all the interruptions of other
Parliamentary bufinefs, may be pronounced
very incompetent to the arduous undertak-
ing. In the courfe of my little correfpondence,

dence, Mr. Editor, I propofe to examine the principles of the bill now before me, and to give an account of the fcope and tendency, the expediency and utility of its feveral claufes. I have no doubt but the Company's cafe (as there treated) will fully appear to be that of a lunatic, who, though not fo frantic as to be deprived of all the benefits and profits of his eftate, is yet confidered as too infane to be entrufted with the management and controul of it. Much do I fear that this legiflative courfe of treatment, fo little adapted to the nature and fymptoms of the malady, will very fpeedily leave the patient no alternative from a ftrait waiftcoat !

DETECTOR.

LETTER II.

Mr. Editor,

IT is a curious but melancholy fpeculation, to trace the flow and infinuating advances of defpotic power: to obferve how an almoft imperceptible change in the fpirit

of

of public meafures, under an affected fcru-
pulofity of adherence to eftablifhed forms,
may gradually undermine the ftrongeft bul-
warks of public liberty. My prefent ad-
drefs is to the proprietors of India ftock;
but my fubject is of confequence to every
chartered body in the kingdom, and to every man who can feel what it is to be a Bri-
ton. Within the laft ten years have the
fubftance and marrow of all the Eaft-India
Company's corporate rights been gently and
unfufpectedly frittered away, under the ap-
pearance of much candid attention to the
privileges of its charters, and a ftudied compliance with the eftablifhed principles of its
inftitution. Every real prerogative, every
folid advantage of independence, hath been
melted down by piecemeal, and abforbed in
the all-grafping influence of the Crown ; in
that influence, which, by a momentary im-
pulfe of exalted patriotifm, the Houfe of
Commons voted to have increafed, to be in-
creafing, and that it ought to be diminifhed.
In that virtuous vote is contained a fure and
perfect antidote againft the pernicious tendency of a bill juft brought into Parliament,
under the fpecious title *of a better regula-*
tion and government of the Britifh poffeffions
in India, and *the fecurity and prefervation*
thereof ; a bill which would diffolve every

tie

tie of public faith, violate every barrier of perfonal and corporate property, annihilate the fecurity of every grant from the legif- lative or executive powers of government, and eftablifh in Afia a fyftem of unlimited tyranny.

" A bill for the better regulation and go- " vernment of the Britifh poffeffions in In- " dia."—Where *are* thefe poffeffions—by whom acquired, and by whom enjoyed?— Certainly by *Britons*—and fo far they are *Britifh* poffeffions. But the poffeffions here alluded to are the fettlements and territories belonging to the Britifh Eaft-India Compa- ny: *private, not national property.* Though I much fear, if this term ' *Britifh poffeffions*' be admitted to pafs in acts of the legiflature, as defcriptive of the Company's eftates, it will (to ufe an elegant legal phrafe), by a fiction of law, covin, engine or deceitful conveyance, ultimately transfer to the Crown a conftructive claim to thofe eftates.

Britifh poffeffions!—The words at the firft fight give an idea of poffeffions attach- ed to and dependent on the Britifh Crown ; in a legal and parliamentary ftyle they can imply nothing elfe. Such are at this day fome few of the Weft-India Iflands, and fuch were at one time the Thirteen Colo- nies of America, now independent. But in
this

this fenfe it is fair and decent to deny that we have any Britifh poffeffions in India— and it will perplex the Crown, and the Crown lawyers, and all the lawyers both of *England* and *Scotland*, to prove that fuch poffeffions exift. I am aware that the prefent bill has but adopted this term from the late regulating and Judicature Acts; that the reports of the Committees, both Secret and Select, thus define the Eaft-India Company's territorial property, and that in ordinary difcourfe the phrafe might pafs unexamined and unfufpected. But it is now time to detect the fallacy, and this is the fpot whereon to make our firft vigorous ftand. A word is enough to the cunning as well as to the wife; and this word ' *Britifh*,' if careleffly admitted as definitive of the India Company's poffeffions, will foon leave it *no poffeffions at all*. The fact is, that fince the 27th of March, 1668, when King Charles the Second ceded Bombay to the Company *for ever*, and fince 16th of December, 1673, when the fame King ceded St. Helena to the faid Company for ever alfo, the Crown has had no property whatever in India, nothing that can with legal precifion be ftyled a *Britifh poffeffion*. Even the 2d claufe of the Bill now before me, betrays the inconfiftency of the term, and

fhews

shews the difficulty under which the framer of it laboured in producing any thing like a plaufible defcription of the *Britifh poffeffions.* It is as follows:—" And whereas, during " the time that the faid United Company " of Merchants of England, trading to the " Eaft Indies, have been in the poffeffion " and enjoyment of the faid whole fole and " exclufive trade to the Eaft Indies, and " parts aforefaid, the faid United Company, " affifted by the fleets and armies of the " King's Majefty, and his Majefty's royal " Predeceffors, have conquered or other- " wife acquired the kingdoms or provinces " of *Bengal, Bahar,* and *Oriffa,* and alfo " certain countries or diftricts fituate on the " coaft of *Coromandel*; and alfo divers other " countries and diftricts in thofe parts " of *Afia,* commonly called the *Eaft In-* " *dies."* It is therefore granted on all hands that the *Company* hath conquered or other- wife acquired the kingdom of Bengal, &c.&c. But it is aledged, ' that they were affifted ' by his Majefty's fleets and armies.' Be it fo. The Company, trading under the fanction and encouragement of a Royal Charter, was clearly in the protection of the Crown, and entitled to its affiftance. In every national war, the Company hath borne its fhare of the public burthen, in common with every other member of the

ftatè, and hath alfo incurred extraordinary
and voluntary expences to an enormous a-
mount in defence of its own property. If
his Majefty's fleets and armies have affifted
the Company in Afia, the very great in-
creafe of revenue to the crown, and of
wealth to the mother country, produced by
the fuccefsful exertions of the Company's
fpirit of enterprize, hath purchafed that affiftance a hundred-fold ; and thofe very
fleets and armies, while in India, are moftly
fupported at the Company's private charge.—
If I regularly contribute my fhare of all the
parochial rates and affeffments, the parifh
muft protect me, in common with the other
inhabitants of the ftreet, by a nightly watch.
The Company have done more : they have
advanced their full proportion of the general affeffments; they have yielded to the
heavieft duties on their trade ; to the moft
diftreffing conditions in all their negociations
with Government; *and have paid the watch-
man alfo.* But even were we to clofe with
the argument adopted by the framer of the
bill, it would be no eafy tafk for him to demonftrate how the affiftance afforded by his
Majefty's fleets and armies, hath fubjected
the poffeffions of the Company to the power
of the Crown. Colonel Clive, with the
Company's own troops, gained the battle of
Plaffey, while the Royal fleet befieged Chan-
dernagore.

'Sernagore. That fettlement, as it was conquered by his Majefty's arms, was given up
by his Majefty's Minifters at the peace. Bengal, Bahar, and Oriffa, are held *not in right
of conqueft* (for the Company reftored them
to the Nabob from whom they had been
taken), but by a *formal deed of ceffion* from
the Emperor of Hindoftan. And to whom
were they ceded? Not to the Crown or Parliament of Great-Britain, but to the Englifh
Eaft-India Company. His Majefty's fleets
and armies were fent to India to protect the
national caufe, againft a national enemy.
What affiftance they might afford to the
Company was on the plea and to the purpofe of diftreffing the French. That formi-
dable antagonift once removed, the Company's footing in the Eaft-Indies became
equally folid and extenfive. After all, I
would not be underftood as dogmatically af-
fecting to pronounce, that the Crown hath
no right to the territorial acquifitions in
Afia; but I affert that as yet there exifts no
public and authoritative Act declaratory of
this right: and that it is beneath the dignity
of the Crown to obtain that prerogative or
influence by a quibbling fubterfuge, which
it hefitates to juftify on a legal and conftitutional foundation. No doubt the firft regulating Act of the 13th of the King, which

F   difpofed

(34)

disposed of near 100,000l. sterling per annum, of the Company's property, in salaries to the Supreme Council and Court of Judicature, without the Company's consent, was a strong symptom of an intended appropriation of the entire property, when occasion should serve. The introduction of the term *British possessions* was another collateral indication of the same design. The term again occurs in the title of the present Bill, and it is now incumbent on the Company to provoke it to a legislative definition. The merits of the Bill are out of the question, until this Preliminary Article shall have been amply and satisfactorily discussed.

LETTER III.

Mr. EDITOR,

THE East-India Company have been long threatened with a parliamentary decision on the right of property to the territorial acquisitions in Asia: and, though the Crown has not yet formally put in its claim, encroachments on the Company's system of

action

action have of late been fo frequent and fo alarming, as fufficiently to demonftrate the fettled defign of a gradual fuperceffion. When every executive function, and every power of controul, fhall have been not only fufpended, but annihilated, the mere phantom of an obfolete title will no longer be worth a ftruggle. Lefs than a dozen years ago, when the chartered privileges of every corporate body were ftill confidered as more than cobweb fecurities---when the times, perhaps, were not ripe for an open avowal of the projected innovations on public faith —the very hint of an attempt to explain away the Company's property in their Afiatic territories, under the clear and literal conftruction of their charter, excited univerfal difcontent. *" Certain ftubborn ideas of law and right,"* (as Mr. Burke was pleafed to ftyle them in a pamphlet, fubfervient to the then *patriotic purpofes.)* were apprehended on the occafion. " Some active perfons of the Company were given to underftand, that this hoftile proceeding was only fet up *in terrorem* ; that Government was far from an intention of feizing upon the poffeffions of the Company. Adminiftration, they faid, was fenfible that the idea was, in every light, full of abfurdity, and that *fuch a feizure was not more out of their power, than*

remote

remote from their wishes." "The original
" plan," which (he says before) "*seems* to
" have been, to get the House of Com-
" mons to compliment the Crown with a fort
" of judicial declaration of a title to the Com-
" pany's acquisitions in India," is now boldly
unmasked: what could not be carried by a
coup de main, has been obtained by flow ap-
proaches in a regular siege ; the outworks
have been all feebly defended, or basely de-
ferted; and the Lord Advocate, on a heap of
ruins, now erects his battery against the laft
tenable quarter.

The whole powers of the Company were
centered in General Courts, and were exercised by the collective body of Proprietors. They elected all their own Directors annually, and considered thofe Directors
but as a *Committee* (by which name they
were originally ftyled in all the charters
of the firft Englifh Eaft-India Company)
of their own body, felected for the difpatch
of bufinefs. They approved or refcinded the
appointment and admiffion of all their own
governors and fervants, and declared their
own dividends on the profits of their own
trade. The independent performance of
thefe feveral acts comprifes almoft the
whole authority which a corporate body can
exercife. Of thefe, former Acts of Parliament,

ment, and ministerial influence together, have already diminished, or defeated the sub-stantial effect, and the Bill now proposed will obliterate the very form. The little controul which at present remains with the General Courts over the resolutions of the Directors, and which is the last relique of their former respectability, is effectually to be abolished by the 32d clause of this new Bill. *" And be it further enacted and de-" clared,* that the several powers and authori-" ties by this Act given to, or vested in, the " said Court of Directors, shall and may from " time to time be exercised, held, and put in " execution by the Directors of the said Uni-" ted Company for the time being, or any " thirteen of them; and *shall not be subject to* " *be rescinded, revoked, altered, varied, affect-* " *ed, or in any respect controuled by the Court* " *of Proprietors, or any of the Proprietors of* " *the said United Company,"* &c. &c. The Di-rectors therefore, or *"any thirteen of them,"* (for these bare majorities are exceedingly convenient for ministerial purposes) are here-by effectually secured from the mortifica-tion of having their measures scrutinised, their motives detected, and their acts re-scinded, by an unmanageable Court of Pro-prietors. No future concurrence of 420 respectable and influenced votes shall here-

after

after oppose and defeat the malicious and
interested combinations of thirteen ill-ad-
vised or corrupted individuals. But, indeed,
no future General Court will probably ever
have a similar occasion, or a similar desire ;
for why should the Company interfere to
serve a slave of the Court, or a tool of
faction, whom they can neither promote,
protect, nor dismiss? By whom, if they are
not betrayed or ruined (and it may possibly
be his interest to do both) they will inevi-
tably be insulted and despised. They will,
indeed, have one consolation, that of seeing
their Directors reduced to their own level
of insignificance; notwithstanding the hu-
miliating terms of this 32d clause, which
too manifestly indicates the foreness of ministerial disappointment on the late virtuous
efforts at the India House. If the General
Courts may no longer revoke, or alter, or
controul the powers and authorities of the
Court of Directors, the Directors themselves
shall be completely manacled and hand-
cuffed in the exercises of those boasted powers and authorities. Their choice of their
own Governor General, and the members
of the Supreme Council, shall be reduced to
a mere *congé d'elire* (clause 27); and they
shall have no power to dismiss any of them,
from their service. (clause 31). For, " in
" case

" cafe the Court of Directors of the faid Uni-
" ted Company, fhall at any time be dif-
" fatisfied with the conduct of any Gover-
" nor General and Captain General of all
" the Britifh fettlements in India, or any of
" the Members of the Council of the *fame*
" *Prefidency*" (meaning, I fuppofe, Calcutta), " and fhall be defirous of his or
" their, or any of their recal or removal, the
" the faid Court of Directors *fhall have full*
" *power and authority*,"—to do what?—
not to order and compel them to obey;
not to fufpend or remove them for difobe-
dience ; not to exercife any of thofe acts
which it is yet conftitutional for them to
refolve, and (with the confent of the Proprietary) to enforce—but " to reprefent the
" fame to his Majefty, his heirs and fuc-
" ceffors, to the intent his Majefty, his heirs
" or fucceffors, may have knowledge there-
" of, and may, upon due confideration and
" advice thereon, *take fuch meafures con-*
" *cerning the fame*, as to his Majefty, his
" heirs or fucceffors, in his or their royal
" wifdom, and juftice, *fhall feem moft fit and*
" *expedient.*" A very confolatory compen-
fation for thofe powers and authorities held
by law under the prefent charter, and fanc-
tioned by Parliament for above eight years
to come!—Thus we may obferve, that, if
the

the Company, in their general and corporate capacity, are laid at the feet of their own Directors, thefe tyrants of the Company are with retributive juftice made to crouch under the throne. One privilege indeed the Directors will lofe by this Act, of which it is impoffible to fay too much, and which I think can hardly be made up to them by the moft liberal extenfion of the prefent mode of conferring contracts, lucrative jobs, and all other minifterial douceurs, whofe value is already fo well afcertained by the able calculators of Leadenhall-ftreet: I mean the chance in which each individual among them now ftands, of becoming Supreme Counfellor, or even Governor General of Bengal. This fyftem of beftowing the chief offices in India on members of the Court of Directors (however liable to be abufed) is moft certainly the next laudable and advantageous expedient to that of fuffering thofe who have ferved a regular gradation of duty through all the Company's fervice abroad, to rife by fucceffion and rotation to feats at the Council-board. But if the new act fhould take place, local knowledge or perfonal experience will operate as decifive difqualifications for ferving the Company; and the firft pretenfions of their fervants, in all their moft confidential and arduous

duous employments, will be *ignorance* and *incapacity.* At prefent, by a very fevere and undeferved ftigma, thofe who have been in the Company's fervice abroad, are prohibited from becoming candidates for the Direction at home, until they fhall have been a year in England; and by the 30th claufe of the new bill, " it fhall not be lawful " for the faid Court of Directors, upon any " vacancy or vacancies which fhall happen " in the refpective offices of Governor " General and Captain General, or Counfel- " lor in the Prefidency of Fort William in " Bengal, or of Governor and Prefident, or " Counfellor in the Prefidencies or Settle- " ments of Madras, Bombay, or Bencoolen, " to nominate any perfon or perfons to fup- " ply any fuch vacancy—or provifionally " appoint any perfon—to fucceed thereto— " refpectively, *who is or are, or fhall be at* " *the time of fuch nomination or appointment,* " *a Director or Directors of the Eaft India* " *Company, or fhall have been a Director*—— " *at any time within the fpace of four years* " *preceding fuch nomination or appoint-* " *ment."*——I fhall expect foon to fee the *Droite d'Aubaine* take place here with re- refpect to thofe unfortunate and profcribed wretches, who have wafted the prime of their lives in the Company's foreign fer-

G vice,

vice. Little elfe remains poffible for them to fuffer.

DETECTOR.

LETTER IV.

Mr. EDITOR,

IN my laft I ftated fome of the imme-diate rights and privileges which the exe-cutive branches of the Company's authori-ty, the Court of Directors, and General Court of Proprietors, would refpectively lofe by the new Bill; as a farther illuftration of the fame fubject, and a more direct proof of the dangerous crifis to which all civil liber-ty is driven by the *principles* of this Bill, I fhall here, in a fummary way, demonftrate the enormous acceffion of power which would from thence accrue to the Crown: under a hope, that thofe whom no other motive can perfuade to behold with the fmalleft candour the dreadful fituation to which the Company are reduced by tyran-nic influence, will at leaft fhudder at the introduction of fo fatal a precedent for other,

and

and more home-felt augmentations of regal prerogative.

The firſt twenty clauſes of the enacting part of the Act, deſcribe the powers, civil and military, to be given to the Governor General, and Captain General of all India; —whom (as I am aware that not being expreſsly appointed to repreſent *Majeſty*, he cannot with propriety be termed *Viceroy)* I ſhall, for the ſake of brevity, and with proper conformity to oriental phraſes and manners, in future, denominate the BASHAW. —In my next letter, I propoſe to take a full ſurvey of his delegated authority, and in the mean time, can aſſure your readers, that no three-tailed minion of the ſublime Porte ever enjoyed a more enlarged, or more deſpotic juriſdiction. This *Baſhaw,* (however nominally and ſpeciouſly he may by the 5th clauſe be made " ſubject—to ſuch orders, " and inſtructions, as he ſhall from time to " time receive from the Court of Directors " of the ſaid united Company,) " it ſhall " and may be lawful to, and for the King's " Majeſty, his heirs and ſucceſſors, by any " writing or inſtrument under the Royal " Seal manual—to be counterſigned by one " of his Majeſty's principal Secretaries of " State, *or otherwiſe, at his or their royal* " *will and pleaſure,* to recal or remove ;"

---as

---as alfo " the Members of the Council
" of Fort William aforefaid, to be at any time
" hereafter appointed;---as alfo all, or any of
" the Governors and Members of the Coun-
" cils of the Prefidencies or fettlements of
" Fort Saint George, Bombay, and Ben-
" coolen, or other Britifh fettlements in In-
" dia, for the time being ; and to vacate, and
" make void all and every, or any appoint-
" ment or appointments, as well abfolute as
" provifional, of any perfon or perfons to
" any of the offices or places aforefaid."
(Claufe 25.)

The reigning Bafhaw, and his Council,
being thus removed by the Fiat of Majefty,
it is provided by the 27th claufe, that the
Court of Directors " immediately after every
" fuch vacancy or recal fhall have been no-
" tified to them, or within 14 days after re-
" quifition fhall be made to them by one
" of his Majefty's principal Secretaries of
" State, fhall proceed to chufe and nominate
" a fit and proper perfon or perfons---to
" fucceed," &c. &c. " and in cafe the per-
" fon or perfons fo chofen *fhall not be*
" *approved by his Majefty*,---then within
" feven days after" (notification thereof)
" the faid Court fhall proceed to chufe and
" nominate fome other perfon or perfons---
" and fo *toties quoties*," until his Majefty
fhall approve of their choice.

By

By this claufe the right of nomination in-
fidioufly and jefuitically, referved to the
Court of Directors, is reduced to a meer
congé d'élire. For if it be allowed that it
is abfolutely neceffary there fhould be any
Governor and Council at all, the Crown
may perfift for ever in rejecting the perfons chofen by the Directors for thofe offices, and the choice muft ultimately fall
on them whom his Majefty fhall be pleafed
to *recommend to be chofen.*—The Crown can
at prefent nominate a judge, or recommend
a Bifhop—but once appointed, they remain
quam diu bene fe gefferint. The Bafhaw of
India is to be created on a more manage-
able plan : and while his powers of defpotifm over fifteen or twenty millions of people will far exceed all authority known to
the Britifh Conftitution, his dependence on
the hand that raifed him, muft be propor-
tionably abject and flavifh ; his office will
become a meer appendage to minifterial liberality, as changeable as the Government
at home, and changing hands regularly
with them : and it will be neceffary for the
Company to have a certain number of packets always lying ready for the annual, or
more frequent recals and re-appointments
of *Whig Bafhaws* and *Tory Bafhaws :* all
nominated *of courfe* by the Directors, and all
approved

approved by his Majefty.----It will not avail the Directors, if they happen by chance, *or on more folid motives*, to wifh for the continuation of their Bafhaw for the time being, to hefitate; and, by feigned or unavoidable delays, procraftinate the nomination of his fucceffor, in hopes that Majefty may relent, or circumftances change in his favour. The 28th claufe debars them of all hope. "In cafe, and fo often as the faid Court " of Directors fhall refufe or neglect to pro-" ceed to any fuch choice and nomination " *within the time aforefaid*" (only fourteen days), " then, and in every fuch cafe, and " fo often as the fame fhall happen, it fhall " be lawful for his Majefty---to conftitute " and appoint---fuch perfons or perfons--- " as his Majefty fhall think proper."----So that, if thirteen Directors can but be perfuaded to perfift for one fortnight in a refufal to nominate their (or rather the Crown's) Bafhaw; or if they fhall not have been able to come to a decided choice within that period, the Royal fign manual fettles the matter at once: and a man whofe very name never reached Leadenhall-ftreet, comes armed with an *imperial firmaun* to demand from them unlimited controul over all their property and all their fervants. If
they

they fhould have forefeen this probable in-
convenience, and wifh to prevent it, by a
timely nomination of provifional fucceffors
to their moft confidential offices, the new
act has even *there* effectually difappointed
them : for fuch provifional nominations
" it fhail and may be lawful" (by the 29th
claufe) " for his Majefty---*without the con-*
" *fent* of the faid Court of Directors, or of
" the faid United Company, to revoke and
" vacate." Indeed, as a very particular
grace, it is liberally permitted the faid Court
of Directors, by the fame 29th claufe, to
annul (" *with the confent of his Majefty, his*
" *heirs, or fucceffors*") thefe their own provifional nominations: and' alfo (*which I
think can never be granted for any good defign or purpofe*) the faid Court of Directors
may give falaries to fuch perfons as fhall
by them be fo provifionally appointed, *before* their becoming entitled to, and taking
upon themfelves the feveral offices, if the
faid Court " *exprefsly order and direct any
" fuch falary to commence and be paid at an
" earlier period, in which cafe the fame fhall
" take place, as the faid Court fhall direct.*"
Who fo blind as not to difcern at leaft half
a dozen Minifterial finecures, *at the Company's expence*, lurking beneath the flimfy
artifice of this paragraph ?---A provifional
Bafhaw,

Bashaw, and his provisional Council, amply provided with *the directions and orders of the said Court* for their provisional salaries, for one, two, three, or any indefinite number of years, hired meerly to give their votes at St. Stephen's, or for some other such laudable service, without the smallest intention in themselves to venture over a ship's side on the Company's account, or in their Masters to emancipate them from domestic drudgery ! ! !

By the 31st clause the Bashaw is rendered compleatly and *ipso facto* independent of all authority whatsoever, as far as the Company or the Court of Directors are any way concerned—and his Majesty is left at full liberty to reject all applications from the said Court of Directors for the removal of the Bashaw or any of his Council, in case the said Court should (on what plea or motive soever) " be dissatisfied with " them, and be desirous of his or their " recal."

The 64th and 67th clauses finally rivet the Company's fetters, as they give to the Crown powers of removing and appointing all the Governors and Counsellors of all the different presidencies and settlements in India, the same in every respect as we have already seen it to be vested with in regard

regard to the Supreme Government of Bengal.

While all the rights and privileges of the East-India Company, as a corporate body united under a Royal Charter, are thus wantonly sacrificed to the prerogative of the Crown, their very property is no less effectually (though in a manner somewhat less glaring) attacked in the 7th clause of the new Act, by the direction of a *new official seal* for the public use of the Bashaw in all his orders, resolutions, proclamations, and other acts of government.

The Company carry on all their official and political correspondence in India, through the hands and in the name of their Governor or President at each settlement respectively: and each Governor or President has (in conformity to the universal and unvaried usage of the Asiatics) a seal engraved in Persian characters, with his name, or titles, or functions (as the case is): and for acts of internal government, the inscription on the seal expresses both the powers of the Company, as Dewan of Bengal, Bahar, and Orissa, &c. &c. and the name of the reigning Mogul Emperor, as paramount of Hindostan. If it were necessary to devise a mode by which the utter annihilation of the Com-

pany's

pany's exiftence fhould at once be clearly
and authoritatively conveyed to the Indian
Princes, and natives of every denomination,
nothing could be fo plaufibly recommended for the purpofe, as a change of the cuf-
tomary feal.——" *Whofe image and fuper-*
"*fcription is this?*" would they fay to
each other, on obferving the uncouth letters and monftrous figures on the new im-
preffion. " What revolution hath taken
" place in the ftamp which ufed to give
" efficacy to all orders, authenticy to all
" devices, and validity to all treaties?"——
The anfwer would confign to perpetual
oblivion, the very name of the Company,
and fuperfede it with that of KING
GEORGE. The application of this feal
(which the Bafhaw is exprefsly ordered by
claufe 22d to carry with him, if he fhould
think it neceffary to go to any or all of the
Company's other fettlements in India, and
to ufe the fame in all public Acts) would
moft emphatically declare to all the Afiatic world, the full affumption of all executive and political powers, in the name and
for the fervice of that Monarch to whom
thofe royal arms appertained.

DETECTOR.

L E T-

LETTER V.

MR. EDITOR,

I Cannot help confidering the propofed
bill, *for regulating the Britifh poffeffions
in India*, as an inftance of moft deliberate
treachery againft all the Principles of our
prefent Conftitution. Every paragraph fup-
preffes the exercife of fome pofitive Chartered Right, or wantonly facrifices fome portion of political freedom. I had flattered my-
felf that my two laft letters contained a full
ftatement of the balance in favour of the
Crown, in the new Account Current with
the Company; but, in the 15th claufe,
(page 10th) I difcover an omitted article,
which alone is fufficient to demonftrate
the iniquitous fcope and purport of the
whole corrupt compofition. " *And be it*
" *further enacted,* That it fhall and may be
" lawful for the faid Governor General,
" and Captain General of all the Britifh fet-
" tlements in India, for the time being, and
" he is hereby authorized and empowered,
" *on behalf of the faid United Company,* and
" IN THE NAME OF HIS MAJESTY,
H 2   " his

" his heirs and fucceffors, from time to
" time, to negotiate and conclude treaties of
" Amity, Peace, *Commerce*, or *Aliance*,
" with any of the Indian Princes or Powers,
" or to declare, make, and levy war againſt
" any Indian Prince or Power, who ſhall
" commence hoſtilities," &c. &c. " againſt
" the Britiſh Nation in India, or againſt any
" of the poſſeſſions, &c. of the ſaid Com-
" pany, or againſt the Subjects, Poſſeſſions
" or Dominions of any Indian Prince or
" Power, whoſe Subjects, &c. the ſaid Com-
" pany ſhall have engaged by any former,
" or ſhall engage by any future Treaty, to
" defend and guaranty." But a war carried on, or a peace concluded, or a treaty
even of commerce negotiated ' *in his Majeſty's*
' *name*,' will not inſpire any Indian Prince
or Power with many favourable ideas of
the Company's reſpectability, or ſeem calculated for any liberal purpoſes, ' *on behalf*
' *of the ſaid Company*.' His Majeſty would
become the principal and ſole Axis of all
political tranſactions in India—and even
the unperceived and imperceptible Rana
of Gohud would treat on equal terms with
the Sovereign of the Britiſh Empire. The
Company, in the mean time, would have
no greater credit or importance in public
affairs, than may be acquired by the ſplen-
did

did employments of forting mulmuls, and weighing falt-petre.

But it is now time to take a nearer furvey of that monfter of defpotifm, *the Bafhaw of all India*; who, like his Proto-types of Bagdad or Aleppo, poffeffing an al-moft abfolute authority over the lives and fortunes of millions, is an abject flave to every paffion or caprice of the power that created him, and can no more difpute a mandate *under the fign manual*, than he can break with impunity his Oath of Alle-giance. By the fifth claufe of the Act, it is provided, that " the whole civil and " military government of the---Prefidency " of Fort William, in Bengal; and alfo " the ordering, management, and govern-" ment of all the---territorial acquifitions " and revenues, and the fuperintendence " and controul, as well *internal as exter-* " *nal,*" (mark that,) " over the refpective " Governors, Prefidents, and Councils of all " the other Prefidencies or Settlements ef-" tablifhed by the faid United Company, " and the Chief Command over all other " Commanders, Captains, Officers, and fol-" diers employed, or to be employed, by " the faid United Company in India, fhall " be, and the fame are hereby vefted in the " ---Governor General and Captain General

" of

" of all the British settlements in India for the
" time being."—This is the grand Patent of
the Bashaw's office, the sum total of his
prerogatives, and the general key to all the
clauses of the Bill. At first sight, it is evident that a military man only can be competent for the discharge of the military part
of the proposed duty, and as such, I hold
him almost necessarily and officially incapacitated for the civil functions of a commercial government, and the minute perplexi-
ties of mercantile affairs.----He is to be af-
sisted (clause 6) by four splendid fantoms,
under the title of Counsellors, whom he
may summons to meet and advise him in
Council from time to time, " *and as often*
" as he shall think fit :" but " if it shall at
" any time happen that the said Governor
" General, and Captain General, shall pro-
" pose any order, resolution, or other act in
" Council, and the major part of the Mem-
" bers, or even all the Members of the said
" Council, shall differ in opinion from him
" concerning the same, and shall refuse their
" consent to the passing thereof.....*and such*
" *Members* (cannot) *be brought to adopt the*
" *opinion of the said Governor General and*
" *Captain General*, then, and in every such
" case---the said Governor General and Cap-
" tain General," (first taking an oath of his
belief

belief of the neceffity of the meafure,) " is " hereby authorized, *by his fole authority*, to " command the fame to be carried into exe- " cution, notwithftanding the diffent of the " Members of the faid Council." (Claufe 13.) —As a proof of his independence as far as concerns the Company, and a badge of fla- very to the Crown, the Bafhaw is to ufe a feal, " bearing the device, fculpture, and re- " prefentation of *his Majefty's Royal Arms*, " within an exergue, or label, furrounding " the fame, with this infcription, " the Bri- " tifh Seal for India." (Claufe 7.)—I have already declared my opinion of the motives which led to the injunction of this new Seal for the political government and corref- pondence, and of the confequences to which it will moft affuredly conduce : I fhall there- fore only add, in this place, that an impref- fion of animals and figures is exceedingly re- pugnant to the cuftoms and religious fyftem of all the Mahomedan inhabitants of India, and argues a very great ignorance of, and in- attention to their prejudices, or an intentional infult on their feelings.— We have feen, by the 13th claufe, an abfolute power given to the Bafhaw, of enforcing any act which he fhall think proper, even againft the advice of all his Council.—The 11th claufe adds to his authority for carrying all his own pro-

pofitions

positions into full effect—that of totally an-
nulling and quashing, *without cause or reason alledged*, all those of his Council, as
" no Act, Resolution, or Order, shall be
" called or deemed (such), or be carried in-
" to execution---without the special consent
" of the said Governor General and Captain
" General." The 16th clause empowers him
" to levy, arm, muster, *command*, and em-
" ploy the armies, troops, and soldiers, in
" the pay of the said Company, in India; and
" in case of invasion, actual or imminent"—
to enforce military law on " *all persons*
" *whomsoever, residing within 'any of the*
" *lands, territories, and dominions, of or be-*
" *longing to, or subject to the government of*
" *the said Company in India*, to resist and re-
" pel, *both at land and sea*, all enemies, pi-
" rates, and rebels, and such to pursue, in or
" out of the limits thereof." By this tyrannous permission, the Bashaw is justified in
forcibly arming all or any part of the Ryots
of Bengal, and in compelling them to take
a sea voyage against the principles of their
cast, and at the certain loss of their lives in a
pertinacious and conscientious refusal of all
nourishment on ship-board, for the purpose
of repelling an invasion in the Northern Circars.---I need be at no farther trouble for ob-
jections. He has also, by the 17th and 18th
claufes,

claufes, authority to feize and imprifon all
perfons fufpected of illicit correfpondence
with Indian or European powers; and, if the
information be upon oath, may fecure and
take into cuftody even the Commanders of
his Majefty's fhips or fquadrons, or any perfons under them, or any Member of the
Supreme Court of Judicature, or any Company's fervant.

It is alfo provided by the 21ft claufe, "that
" from and after the commencement of this
" Act, all and fingular the Governors, and
" Prefidents, and Councils of all the towns,
" forts, factories, prefidencies, and fettle-
" ments, which now are, or hereafter may
" be erected or eftablifhed by the faid Com-
" pany in India, fhall be dependent upon
" and fubordinate to the fuperintending and
" controuling power of the faid Governor
" General and Captain General of all the
" Britifh fettlements in India, *in all cafes*
" *whatfoever*, civil and military, refpecting
" the government and adminiftration of their
" refpective governments and fettlements;"
and " if, at any time hereafter, any dan-
" gerous commotion fhould arife, or fla-
" grant mifmanagement be committed,"
(claufe 22,) at any of the fubordinate fettlements, the Bafhaw " may, in perfon, repair
" to fuch prefidency or fettlement, *taking*

I   " *with*

" *with him the feal aforesaid*," and on Pro-
clamation being made of his arrival, " all
" the power and authority of the Governor,
" President, and Council thereof, shall be
" suspended, and the whole and sole order-
" ing, management, and government of
" the said subordinate presidency or settle-
" ment shall be vested in the said Governor
" General and Captain General, so long as
" he shall there remain." He may also dif-
miss and send to Europe the former President and Council, and appoint others provi-
sionally in their places.—I must here remark, that when the 13th of the King first
took place in India, and a majority of the
Supreme Council of Bengal came from
England to govern the political concerns of
India, without having passed through the
several gradations of employment in the
Company's service, it was judged highly
necessary for the interest and well-doing of
the Company, that a Board of Trade should
be established of such of the Company's
civil servants as, being senior in rank, had
naturally acquired most experience and knowledge in the several branches of the Company's commerce ; these were to have the
whole and sole management of all the Company's mercantile transactions in Bengal ; for
attention to which the Supreme Council
were

were fuppofed inadequate, from the multitude and intricacy of their financical and political fpeculatións, as well as incapacitated by an utter inexperience in commercial matters.—This Board of Trade (for aught that appears to the contrary in the new Act) it is ftill propofed to retain, and therefore the new Bafhaw and his Council would ftill, in Bengal, be debarred by law as well as by habit from giving any attention to the rules, or principles, or practices of the Company's trade. But by this 22d claufe, whenever the Bafhaw fhall judge it expedient to take his perfon and his feal to Madras, Bombay, or Bencoolen, he becomes paramount in commerce as well as in politics, and controuls the Company's inveftment with as little ceremony as he contradicts his own Council.

We have feen above, that, by the 13th claufe, the Bafhaw (on taking an oath) may enforce any Act or Refolution of his own, againft the advice and confent of all his Council : and, by the 11th claufe, that without an oath he may quafh every propofition of his Counfellors by the meer witholding of his confent. It fhould therefore feem, that by thefe two claufes the power of the Bafhaw was extended to every thing that can be called reafonable or decent in any fpecious

I 2   fyftem

syftem of government, and the oftenfible
functions of the Counfellors debafed as low
as any man with a fpark of human feeling
about him could fubmit to degrade himfelf
by accepting.—But by the 23d claufe, we
may remark a refinement of defpotifm well
worthy of Afiatic invention: as the Bafhaw is
there inftructed how, without the trouble or
expence of an oath in the one cafe, or the
mortification of putting a negative on the
wifhes of his Council in the other, he
may exercife his double prerogative at Calcutta in its whole extent, and take his full
fwing of political authority, joined to an
efficient and irrefiftable fway over all the
official departments of Commerce at fome
fubordinate fettlement into the bargain. I
muft therefore once more intrude (Mr.
Editor) on the patience of your readers, for
fomewhat of a long quotation, which I offer
as a hint to the new Bafhaw never to refide
in Calcutta ; and to his Council never to be
at the fatigue of advifing, or the refponfibi-
lity of executing any meafure of Government, but to pocket, as quietly as may be, the
miferable wages of their own infignificance.
—(Claufe 23) '' And be it further enacted,
'' that when and fo often as the faid Gover-
'' nor General and Captain General fhall be
'' abfent from the faid Prefidency of Fort
'' William,

" William, either upon his vifitation of any
" of the fubordinate Settlements, or other
" occafion, the ordering, management, and
" government of the faid Prefidency fhall
" remain in, and be exercifed by the other
" Members of the Council remaining at
" Fort William, in Bengal," &c. &c. ---
" *Subject neverthelefs to fuch orders as they*
" *fhall have previoufly received, or may*
" *from time to time receive, from the faid*
" *Governor General and Captain General of*
" *Bengal for the time being."*
D E T E C T O R.

L E T T E R VI.

Mr. Editor;

THAT part of the new *Bill for the better regulation and government of the
Britifh poffeffions in India,* of which I have
in my laft letters difplayed the dangerous tendency and purport, fully authorifes my firm
conviction that the whole will be unani-
moufly rejected by the Legiflature with more
than ordinary marks of fcorn and detefta-
tion.

(62)

tion. An attempt to veſt in the Crown the ſole appointment and diſmiſſion of all the Governors, Preſidents, and Counſellors employed in the Company's ſervice in India, and by theſe means the entire controul and diſpoſal of all that property holden by the Company in right both of its Charter and of repeated Acts of Parliament, will certainly excite very ſtrong ſenſations in thoſe who wiſh to preſerve the general balance of our preſent Conſtitution. A covert and indirect invaſion of the Company's poſſeſſions, without the proof or even the pretext of any legal claim, while it betrays a dirty pettifogging meanneſs of impoſition, that would diſgrace both the parts and the conſcience of a beggarly attorney, will, without doubt, be ſtrongly reprobated by all who foreſee the conſequences of innovations on chartered and parliamentary ſecurities. Thoſe who deprecate the increaſe of venal and corrupt influence in our Government, will aſſuredly oppoſe ſo great an addition to Miniſterial importance, as would be acquired by the arbitrary means of gratifying twenty more dependents with moſt lucrative appointments abroad, and of granting proviſional ſalaries (clauſe 29) to five others at home. Men, who with a more extenſive liberality of ſentiment feel for the cauſe of general liberty, and

and look beyond national prejudices to a
confideration for the common independence
of mankind, will be interefted by 'the moft
exalted of human paffions, fympathy for the
fituation of feveral millions of Afiatics, as well
as fome hundreds óf their own countrymeh,
expofed to all the worft effects of avarice,
ignorance, caprice, or brutality, in a delegated tyrant, for whofe acts of *legal* defpotifm the quickeft poffible termination cannot be hoped in lefs than fix months, and
who, at the bare peril of an oath, is *autho-
rifed* to take upon himfelf the perpetration
of every enofmity that human invention
can fuggeft. Thefe being the oftenfible and
incontrovertible principles of the new Bill,
have required neither art nor induftry to
difplay them in their proper colours.—
But as I do not fufpect it to have much
chance of attaining to any active powers of
exiftence, I fhould think it an unpardonable
trefpafs on the public, were I, in the prefent
ftage of the bufinefs, to diffect with fo much
minutenefs of attention as I have hitherto
employed, the other objectionable Members
that ftill obtrude themfelves on my notice. I
already difcern ample materials for a dozen
letters were they yet neceffary, on the eight
claufes from the 40th to the 47th inclufive:
—On the certain feeds of future contention
                                    fown

fown in the new powers intended for the
Supreme Court ; in the *"active as well as de-*
*" liberative voice "*given to the Judges equally with the Supreme Council, for making
and iffuing " fuch rules, ordinances, and
" regulations, as fhall be deemed juft and
" reafonable for the good order and civil
" government of the faid kingdoms of Ben-
" gal, Bahar, and Oriffa, and *of the coun-*
" tries or diftricts fituate on the coaft of
" Coromandel, known by the name of the
" Northern Circars" (to which the power or
influence of the Supreme Court of Judicature at Calcutta has never yet had the fhadow
of a claim), " and of all other Countries and
" Diftricts in India, which now are or here-
" after may be fubjected *to the government*
" and controul of his Majefty, or of the faid
" united Company : *and alfo for the better*
" ordering, management, and government of
" the territorial acquifitions and revenues,
" and all other rents,-profits and revenues
" arifing and growing due to the faid Com-
" pany within the fame, or any of them :
" and alfo for the affefling and levying---
" reafonable taxes and impofitions-----and
" alfo duties of export, import and tranfit,
" on all goods, wares, and merchandifes."--
&c. &c. — How far, I fay, thefe very un-
ufual *fifcal functions* beftowed on the Judges
may

may fuit the interefts of the Company, or
contribute to the benefit of the ftate, may
be left as a fubject not ripe, nor likely to
ripen, for difcuffion. From thence to the
8oth claufe (except fo much as relates to the
new mode of appointing Governors and
Counfellors to the fubordinate fettlements)
is but a fuperceffion of powers already granted to the Company by former Acts and Charters, or a recapitulation of orders even now
in force, or affected refinements on the late
and former Judicature Acts. — How the
Framer of the 8 1ft claufe, which recommends
the eftablifhment of falaries in the revenue
department on a liberal plan, " *as a fatif-*
" *faction for the due and punctual perform-*
" *ance of that duty,*" will reconcile his propofition here quoted, to that of the 89th
claufe, which enacts, that lifts of all the
civil and military offices and employments
fhall be fent home, accompanied with
fchemes of œconomy, and advices how the
fame may be better regulated, &c. &c. is
not for me to explain. Sure I am, that repeated efforts for "retrenching unneceffary
" expences, and for introducing a juft and
" laudable œconomy in every branch of the
" civil and military fervice," have already
been exerted as far as reafon, juftice, and the
comparative duties of different ftations,

K. and

and neceſſary gradations of rank and precedence will admit. Expences may be thrown into different forms, emoluments may be transferred to new channels, plauſible pretences may introduce flattering innovations,—but the real and ultimate charge to the public is already as low as the public ſervice will bear. If Acts of Parliament ſhall continue to confer enormous ſalaries in pounds ſterling to new Governors and Counſellors, and to give a licence (not likely to grow obſolete for want of application) to the Court of Directors for granting other proviſional ſalaries to proviſional Governors, &c. *all out of the Company's pocket*, the ſum total of expenditure will certainly and neceſſarily increaſe, in ſpite of the moſt jealous and illiberal ſcrutiny into all the little perquiſites and eſtabliſhed emoluments of office in India. In theſe caſes, what individuals may loſe will be infinitely beyond all proportion of what the public can poſſibly gain : and I affirm, with the utmoſt confidence, that more than what can be ſubtracted from ſuch emoluments will and muſt (even by the very reaſoning of the 81ſt clauſe) be added to ſalaries.—I ſhall now juſt ſlightly run over the concluding clauſes, *thoſe fringes of the bill*, and for the preſent take my leave ;

not

not without pledging myself to go into the merits of each particular article, should the mongrel fœtus of servility and despotism fail to be stifled in its birth. An Act intended for the benefit of our Asiatic fellow-creatures, should be the result of much dispassionate reflection, philosophical experience, and disinterested philanthropy. While the causes of our calamities in India are so miserably misunderstood and so shamefully misrepresented, every new political prescription adds to the complication of disorders. What substantial wisdom or sound policy can be discerned in visionary schemes for the restoration of dispossessed Rajas and Zemindars, or a restitution of their old feudal authority and jurisdiction (and that too under the sanction of a British Act of Parliament !) ? (clause 82) as if the ridiculous canting proposals for restoring " the said dominions to their antient " state of splendor and opulence" by such frothy projects, had really been *proved*, as well as " *represented to the High Court of Parliament.*"——The 83d clause argues a profound ignorance of the internal state of the Country Government, with respect to the Revenue, or else (which is as little admissible in an Act of the Legislature) the words " Phougdarree Court" are *by mistake* inserted for the Words " Court of Dewanny A-

K 2   " daulet,

" daulet," and at all events it militates a-
gainft the jurifdiction propofed by the 82d
claufe to be reftored to the Zemindars.—
The 84th claufe is an echo to the 44 Refolutions of the Secret Committee, as far
as they tend to reprobate the purfuit of
" Schemes of Conqueft and Extent of Do-
" minion :" viz. thofe very points, on which
the refolutions themfelves failed to imprefs
conviction on any well-informed mind.
Schemes of Conqueft, and a wifh to extend
our Dominion, are ideas perfectly diftinct :
they have indeed both been imputed to
Governor General Haftings, and both in
every inftance *have been repeatedly, can be
at prefent,* and *fhall be at any and every future
period,* folemnly difavowed, and fatisfactorily
difproved *upon full and authentic teftimony.*
Let the learned Framer of the Bill ftep forward, and produce his *vouchers* that Mr.
Haftings hath ever " *wilfully* adopted or
" countenanced a Syftem tending to infpire
" a reafonable Diftruft of the Moderation,
" Juftice, and good Faith of the Britifh Na-
" tion"—and I affure him the charge fhall
be formally and pointedly refuted. Thefe
affertions, I own, are vague, but none elfe
can be adapted to his prefent vague futile
and general accufations. When he has
eftablifhed his feveral Criminatory Articles,

Of

or when the metaphoric Orator on the other
fide of the houfe (who, like an unruly ele-
phant, cannot be trufted in public without
a camel on each fide to keep him in order,)
has reduced his erratic hyperboles to *plain
reafon* and *matter of fact*, then, and then
only, will be the proper time for fpecioufly
bringing forward a Bill to remove the Author of the Mahratta Peace, and the Saviour
of the Carnatic.

The debts of the Nabob of Arcot, and
thofe of the Raja of Tanjore (including, I
fuppofe, the fums borrowed to pay his A-
gents and Embaffadors refidentiary) are required by the 86th and 87th claufes to be
inveftigated, which furely did not need the
interference and exprefs injunction of an Act
of Parliament. An order from the Court of
Directors might at leaft be competent to
their examination, tho' perhaps affiftance
might be wanting to enforce their liquida-
tion. I had almoft forgotten the 85th claufe,
which fanctions the independence of the Raja
of Tanjore by Parliament *(no parliamentary
enquiry having taken place on the fubject)*,
on the principles recommended to, and
adopted by Lord Pigot.

I fhall now take the privilege of an old
correfpondent to leave off abruptly and without ceremony. While India matters are the
fubject

subject of discussion, and particularly so long
as one of the most respectable characters
in the British Empire *shall be wantonly and
injuriously* attacked, you, Mr Editor, and
the public, may expect occasionally to hear
from

DETECTOR.

May 10, 1783.

OBSERVATIONS

Observations *on the* Eighth Report *of the* Select Committee.

AT the conclusion of the Rohilla War in 1774, a Treaty was made between the late Vizier of Oude, and Fyzoolah Khan, one of the Rohilla Chiefs — whereby the latter, on certain conditions, was put into the poffeffion of Rampore, and fome other diftricts in the Rohilla Country (8 Report, page 18) as a Jagheer for the amount of 1475000 Rupees per annum (page 4). In 1778, the Company (through their Refident at the Court of the prefent Vizier) became Guarantees to this Treaty (page 9). In September, 1781, the Governor General of Bengal, in a new Treaty of Alliance between the Company and the Vizier, affented to a modification of this Guarantee : by which the Vizier was to be permitted, at fome future period, to refume the ceded lands, on condition of paying the annual ftipulated amount of the Jagheer from his own Treafury, through the hands of our Refident. But as the Governor General apprehended fome political inconveniencies both to the Company and the Vizier from this propofed

Refumption

Refumption of the Jagheer lands, he referved the actual execution of that Article in the new Treaty to an indefinite term, fubject to the future interpofition of our Government. (Page 17.)

This is the outline of *'the Cafe'* which the Select Committee have thought it their Duty to reprefent to the Houfe in their Eighth Report, and on which they appear to have implicitly adopted the general and particular cenfure expreffed by the Court of Directors in their general Letters to Bengal, dated 12 July, 1782, and 14 Feb. 1783. (Pages 18, 19, and 20.)

" To procure and maintain the peace of
" India—to quiet the Fears of the neigh-
" bouring Powers, who, from the Conduct
" of our Servants, have had too much reafon
" to be jealous of our Encroachments—to
" adhere ftrictly to Treaties, and never to be
" the aggreffors—to fecure to the Natives
" under the immediate Government of the
" Country the undifturbed Exercife of their
" Religion and Cuftoms, and to encourage
" Cultivation, Manufactures, and Com-
" merce—are the means by which we hope
" to regain the Confidence of the Native
" Princes, and the Attachment of the Peo-
" ple. By fuch means, and by fuch alone,
" we may hope to fee our affairs once more
" flourifh

" flourifh, and Permanency *again* given to
" the Company's Poffeffions in the Eaft-
" Indies."

In the canting philanthropy of this plaufible paragraph, the Select Committee feem to
have difcovered a moft fevere and pointed
Arraignment of the Governor General's
Conduct in the *Cafe* above related. For my
own part, I can only difcern in it fuch a
heterogeneous jumble of internal adminiftration with external politics, fuch general and
indefinite references to the *Whole of India,*
as if it were all comprifed under one univerfal fyftem of Government, and actuated by
the fame common plan of policy, that fo
far from containing Cenfure, I doubt if it
can ever be ftrained into meaning.

" *To procure and maintain the Peace of*
" *India,*" we ought certainly to be Paramount, and muft neceffarily interfere in all
the difputes among the Indian Princes; but
this is diametrically the reverfe of that Conduct which our Governments are inftructed
to purfue. " *To quiet the fears of the Neigh-*
" *bouring Powers,*" and particularly to obviate the " *Reafons* they have *to be jealous of*
" *our Encroachments,*" we muft withhold
every degree of influence in the interior
management of the refpective Territories of
thofe Powers : and yet we cannot poffibly
L   " fecure

" fecure to the Natives, under the *immediate*
" *Government of the Country,* the *undifturbed*
" exercife of their Religion and Cuftoms,"
(whatever we may to thofe under the immediate Government of the *Company)* without continual and very ftrenuous exertions
of authority over the immediate Government of that Country whofe Natives we
would thus fecure.—If we encourage *Commerce,* we need be in no pain about the *Cultivation* and *Manufactures.* They will im-
prove of courfe. But if any other *Encouragement* be here implied, it can certainly
take place only in thofe Territories over
which the Company exercife an exclufive
Jurifdiction.—" The means by which we
" may hope to regain *the Confidence of the Na-
" tive Princes"* are furely very different from
thofe which we muft purfue to acquire " *the*
" *Attachment of the People."* For the firft
object, we are bound to be cautious in the
extreme, left we afford a pretext for difobe-
dience, or fupport any prefumptuous pretenfions in the Subjects of any Native Power
towards their Sovereign, either by the perfonal protection of a Refident, or the public Authority of a Guarantee. If therefore,
under the plea of " fecuring to the Natives"
(fuch, I mean, as are not our own immediate
fubjects) " *the undifturbed Exercife of their*
" *Religion*

" *Religion and Cuſtoms*," we officiouſly obtrude our own ideas and principles of relative and diſtributive Juſtice, as Rules of
Action for the Country Powers in the Exerciſe of their own Dominion over their
own Subjects ; if we are for preſcribing
the meaſure of Obedience due from the
Vaſſal to his Lord; and, on the pretence of
protecting the people, avowedly exert an
unlimited Controul over the Prince, we
ſhall never " regain the Confidence of the
" native Princes," nor (except by the Jus
fortioris) " procure and maintain the Peace
" of India."

Upon the whole, this moral and benevo-
lent Paragraph can but at moſt be conſtru-
ed to expreſs the Senſe of the Court of Directors, that it would be good policy in
their Governments abroad to exerciſe a liberal and lenient Juriſdiction over their own
Territories, and to concern themſelves as
little as poſſible with thoſe of their neigh-
bours.

" It is exceedingly proper," ſay the Court
of Directors, in the Paragraph immediately
preceding that which I have juſt analyſed,
" that your Government ſhould ſee that Fy-
" zoolah Khan fulfills his Engagement with
" the Vizier, according to the Treaty guaran-
" teed by the Company."—Much as this

acute

acute obfervation muft have coft of deep
and painful thinking to the Four and Twenty Directors, it would not have been labour
ill-beftowed to have gone a ftep farther,
by confidering *how* the Government was to
fee this Engagement fulfilled : for the whole
of the queftion feems to me to turn upon
the Mode of Conduct proper to be adopted
upon this Occafion.   For inftance, if Fyzoolah Khan were under the acknowledged
Government of the Company, *their Orders*
muft be deemed fufficient to bring him to a
Senfe of his Duty.   If he were a Subject
of the Vizier, by withdrawing our Guarantee, on proof of his violation of the Treaty,
*we quieted the Fears of a Native Prince on
the Extent of our Encroachments,* and left
the Sovereign at liberty to vindicate his own
rights by his own powers.   If Fyzoolah
were an independent Prince, *fui Juris,* we
had no alternative, fhould he perfift in a refufal to perform the Articles of his Agreement, but to join our forces to thofe of the
Vizier, and reduce him to a neceffity of
compliance, under the terms of the Guarantee.

As this moft effential part of the enquiry
feems to be involved in a ftudied obfcurity,
or at leaft to have been carelefsly overlook-
ed, I fhall take the liberty to examine it under

der the five following heads; from which, I doubt not, but we fhall extract fomething of a decifive and fatisfactory elucidation of the whole bufinefs.

1. What were the original relative fituation, views and interefts of the two contracting parties?

2. For what purpofe, and to what extent, did the Company annex their Guarantee to the Engagements between the Vizier of Oude, and the Rohilla Chief?

3. Was the Treaty, to which the Company were Guarantees, actually violated, or implicitly fulfilled?

4. How far can the Company, with propriety, interfere in fuch cafes, and in this particular Cafe?

5. For what caufe, and to what end, did the Governor General of Bengal enter into the new Treaty with the Vizier?

With refpect to the firft Article, the original Treaties are fo loofe and indefinite, at leaft the Tranflation is fo extremely fhort of precifion, that it is very difficult from thence to form an accurate idea of the footing on which the Vizier and the Rohilla Chief refpectively ftood at the moment of their mutual agreement. The Vizier, in *his* part of the Treaty, is made to fay, " A *Friend-* " *fhip* having been entered into between me " and Fyzoolah Khan:" The other party re-

turns

turns the same form of phrase, " A *Friend-* " *ship* hav ng taken place between the Na- " bob Vizier ul Mulk Behader and me." So far they appear to treat on terms of equality, reciprocal obligation, and . mutual independence : and it is only to a negocia- tion between parties of such a defcription that the term " Treaty" can with proprie- ty be applied. Col. Champion makes no ufe of this word in his public letter (p. 4). He expreffes himfelf by the terms " *agree-* " *ment*" and " *engagement*," which leave the nature of the political connection between the ftipulators perfectly undefined : They are however entirely confiftent with the re- lative ftates of *fovereign* and *fubject*, while a *Treaty* can only take place where there is no immediate dependence and acknowledged fubjection. The Counterpart of the Agree- ment, on the part of Fyzoolah Khan, effec- tually clears up the doubt, by a full and im- plicit avowal of his own inferiority, and, in terms that cannot be mifunderftood, pro- mifes the allegiance of a fubject. " I will " always, whilft I live, continue in *fubmiffi-* " *on* and *obedience* to the Vizier :" and far- ther on, " *Whatever the Nabob Vizier di-* " *rects, I will execute.*" This furely is not the language of a *Treaty*; it is a plain profeffion of Fealty. And if we became fureties to Fyzoolah Khan for the

the due enjoyment of his Jagheer on the one part, we certainly, on the other, guranteed to the Vizier a continuance of submiffion and obedience from the Rohilla Chief, and a punctual execution of all his orders.——As the mere poffeffion of a Jagheer moft indifputably does not emancipate the Jagheerdar from the condition of a fubject in other refpects, and ftill lefs confers the powers and privileges of fovereignty, it was a great overfight in the Court of Directors and the Select Committee to adopt Mr. D. Barwell's inaccurate mode of expreffion, in calling Fyzoolah Khan's renters or ryotts " *his Subjects*," (page 18.) whereas he and they were in common Subjects to the Vizier, as is amply proved by Fyzoolah's own ftipulation.——When the Jagheer was firft granted to the Rohilla Chief, it was exprefsly valued at 1475000 Rs. * but a better knowledge of the country arifing from the keennefs of examination excited by the Vizier's

* I have examined the Records of the Bengal Government for the year 1774, and find that the propofed Jagheer was augmented from 1200000 to 1475000, by the ftrong interpofition of Col. Champion, and granted with much reluctance by the late Vizier: on Fyzoolah Khan's moft earneft reprefentation, that 1200000 would be abfolutely infufficient to afford a mere comfortable fubfiftence to his Relations and immediate Dependents.

Vizier's pecuniary diftreffes, has fince difcovered the produce to have been greatly
(and, it is folemnly urged, fraudulently)
under-rated. Moft affuredly the Company's guarantee cannot, by any latitude or
partiality of conftruction, be made to extend
beyond the fettled amount of 1475000 Rs.
and if more had been obtained *by falfe pretences*, I fee neither juftice nor plaufibility
in our interference to prevent the Vizier
from refuming the Overplus. It muft be
remembered, that a *Jagheer* in India is pre-
cifely the fame as a *Fief* under the feodal
Syftem, and in the fame manner ufually
held by *military tenure :* that is, fuch a
portion of land is deemed adequate to the
maintenance of fo many Troops, and the
Land-holder is bound to bring that number into the field on every requifition of the
Sovereign. When Fyzoolah Khan's Jagheer was firft granted, the peculiarity of his
fituation dictated fome peculiar claufes in
the grant. While he was a new fubject to
the Vizier, and while the Rohillas, his
countrymen, might be fuppofed to retain a
ftrong fpirit of revenge for their Loffes, and
had even yet the means of becoming formi-
dable, if united, it was prudence and policy
to obftruct by every cautionary expedient
the very poffibility of their union. Therefore,

fore, while other feodal dependents are exprefsly held to furnifh a certain quota of Troops, it was only ftipulated with Fyzoolah Khan, that he fhould *not* entertain *a fingle man more than* 5000 in his fervice. His allegiance was at that time confidered as fufpicious; and the object was not fo much to render his affiftance ufeful, as his oppofition fruitlefs. But whatever hopes of aggrandizement or independence Fyzoolah Khan might have cherifhed in the early part of his fubmiffion, it is clear, that, after the death of Sujah Dowla, he was only anxious to eftablifh himfelf againft that mutability of fortune which is congenial to all Afiatic governments. We know that in Turkey, in Perfia, in Hindoftan, and wherever the principles of the feodal fyftem have been blended with defpotic power in the Sovereign, the only fecurity of the throne feems to confift in the fudden elevations and removals of the feveral afpirers to rank and dignity in the State. Jagheers are granted and refumed, great employments are conferred on obfcure men, and the firft officers of the State degraded, or banifhed, or put to death, with a promptitude of decifion, difregard of formalities, and indifference of perfons, utterly incompatible with the liberality and refinement of

M   modern

modern European manners. It muft certainly therefore be more than commonly
grating to the Vizier, to feel the pervad-
ing Influence of Britifh interference in the
internal management of his own concerns,
It muft leffen his dignity in the eyes of
every native Prince, and militate againft
all his own notions óf the rights and functions of Sovereignty, to be oppofed and
thwarted in executing his own purpofes
upon his own Subjects by the interpofition pf a foreign guarantee.

This will naturally lead us to the fecond
head of enquiry as to the purpofe and extent of the Company's Guarantee in the
prefent cafe. Col. Champion's original letter on the firft outfet of the bufinefs, expreffes the matter in two lines: "Fyzoolah
"Khan is to have a Jagheer of 1475000
"Rs. in the Rohilla Country, with liberty
"to keep 5000 men in arms." (Page 4.)
"Fyzoolah, in return, was to continue in
"fubmiffion and obedience to the Vizier,
"and execute whatever he directed."
(Page 5.) The Company were not, by this
Guarantee, bound to fecure to Fyzoolah
a revenue of 30 Lacs inftead of 14, nor to
eftablifh for him an independent Jurifdiction over the lards which he held on the
common tenure of any other Jagheer, nor to
defeat

defeat and render null the conditions of obedience and submission in which he pledged himself to the Vizier. We find that before the concession of the Guarantee, jealousies and mistrust had arisen in both parties. The Vizier suspected Fyzoolah Khan of an intention to throw off his dependence: " It is not impossible" (says the Company's Resident at Lucknow) " but he" (Fyzoolah) " might be induced to form " connections, and to engage in schemes, " incompatible with his duty and *allegiance* " to the Vizier." (Page 5.) On the other hand, he observes, that Fyzoolah Khan, " having heard of the acts of injustice and " oppression which the Vizier is constantly " exercising upon those who are wholly at his mercy," was apprehensive that his country should be seized, and himself involved in ruin. (Page 6.) How much soever the Vizier might wish to act up to Fyzoolah Khan's apprehensions, he has hitherto refrained from every thing that could be construed into a deviation from his engagements: but he has loudly, and on plausible grounds, complained of infractions of the Conditions on the other part. His Letter to Mr. Haftings (page 17) states that the excess of Collections in the Jagheer is " *proved to demonstration*" to have been a

M 2 *fraud*

fraud in the firſt valuation, inſtead of the produce of an increaſed cultivation. What collateral proofs the Vizier might have obtained, we are not informed : but ſuch is the poſitive and authoritative Report of Mr. Johnſon, an Envoy deputed jointly from the Vizier and the Company's Reſident to the Capital of the ceded Lands. " *Fyzoolah* " *Khan's exceſs of revenue,*" ſays he, " *lays in* " *a fraudulent valuation at the time of the* " *Grant.*" (Page 15.) In the next place, Mr. Johnſon, in his public capacity, and in an official letter, pointedly and unconditionally aſſerts, that " at this moment there " are not leſs than 20000 Rohilla Soldiers in " the diſtrict of Rampore alone."——" *Upon* " *this Clauſe the Grant runs, and is of courſe* " *forfeited.*" (Page 16.) When we recollect that all the late Vizier's policy was exerted, at the time of his firſt agreement with Fyzoolah Khan, to prevent any dangerous acceſs of numbers to his new Subject's ſtandard : that out of the preſent Vizier's Jealouſy on the ſame account, aroſe the Deputation of Mr. D. Barwell, before whom Fyzoolah Khan was content to cauſe near 5000 Troops to be muſtered, which Mr. Barwell *found to fall rather ſhort of the number ſpecified in the Treaty* (p. 7): and that Mr. Johnſon now affirms upwards of 20000

to

to be In Rampore only, it muſt ſeem a little extraordinary that the Court of Directors ſhould write (p. 20), " *We can no where* " *diſcover that Fyzoolah Khan has been guilty* " *of a Breach of Treaty.*" But this is not all. Fyzoolah Khan was reſtricted, it is true, to 5000 men ; and on " the 2d day of " November, 1780, the Governor General " and Council, in their ſecret department, " agreed " that the Governor General be " requeſted to write to the Nabob Vizier, " recommending to him to require from " Fyzoolah Khan the quota of Troops ſti- " pulated by Treaty to be furniſhed by the " latter for his Service, being *five thouſand* " *horſe.*" (Page 12.) Fyzoolah Khan re- turned for anſwer, that the 5000 men al- lowed him, conſiſted, according to his ori- ginal aſſignments for their Expences, " *of* " 2000 *horſe,* and 3000 *foot.*" (Page 13.) That Fyzoolah Khan could not furniſh Troops which did not exiſt is very certain : nor is he blamed for it. But he ſhould have *offered to raiſe them,* or at leaſt to mount his 3000 Infantry, which would have been ſufficient, if he wiſhed to demonſtrate his " *continuance in ſubmiſſion and obedience to* " *the Vizier;*" and in neglecting to make ſuch offer, he moſt indiſputably "*evaded the* " *performance of his part of the Treaty,*" as

ſtated

ftated by the Governor General in his minute. (Page 13.) To compromife the matter, to gratify in fome degree Fyzoolah's pertinacity without too public a degradation of the Vizier's authority ; to patch-up, in fhort, this late *evafion* of the Treaty ere it fhould amount to an abfolute Breach, was the object of Mr. Johnfon's miffion. As on the one hand Fyzoolah's offer ftated 2000 Cavalry, and the original demand had required 5000—there is an evident conceffion and wifh to accommodate the difpute, in fending peremptorily to "*demand immediate* " *delivery of* 3000 *Cavalry*" only. (Page 14.) To this injunction Fyzoolah Khan anfwered by "*a flat Refufal*" (page 16) : the very Fyzoolah who had " fworn on " the holy Koran, calling God and his Pro- " phets to witnefs, " *that whatever the Na-* " *bob Vizier directs, I will execute.*"(Page 5.)

Having now, as I think, brought the proof of a direct violation of the Treaty to irre- futable demonftration, I would afk how far the Company can, with propriety, interfere, as guarantees, to exact a due performance of the Articles, or to punifh the Infraction ? " It is exceedingly proper," fay the Court of Directors, in their General Letter to Ben- gal (page 18), " That your Government " fhould *fee* that Fyzoolah Khan fulfils his " engage-

" engagement with the Vizier." The other part of the Sentence shews them to have considered the Rohilla Chief as an independent Prince; and I have above amply proved the contrary from Fyzoolah's own words. " But we wish," say they, " rather to be " considered as the Guardians of the Ho- " nour and Prosperity of the native Powers " of India with whom we are in any degree " connected, than as the Instruments of Op- " pression: we hope and trust, therefore, " that no hostile steps have been taken " against the Rohilla Chief."

Fyzoolah Khan is no *native power*, in the sense there applied; he is a subject to the Vizier, guaranteed by us in the possession of lands to a stipulated amount, on certain conditions. If he hath broken those conditions, we surely do not become *the instruments of oppression*, by leaving him to the laws of his country, or the mercy of his own Sovereign. The Vizier would have infinitely more *reason to be jealous of our encroachments*, had we pretended to take the powers of executive justice out of his hands, and to punish according to our system of Government, or at our own discretion, *his* subjects for a failure of allegiance to *him*. This would be crying out in too loud a strain, " You shall be King, " but We will be Vice-Roy over you." In

fact,

fact, from the inftant that Fyzoolah Khan
forfeited his claim to the Guarantee by a
breach of his engagement, our connections
with him virtually ceafed. He became to all
intents and purpofes amenable to his Sovereign the Vizier, and to him alone. *Policy,*
perhaps, might incline us to ftand between
Fyzoolah Khan, and that wrath which
would " leave him to join his other faith-
" lefs Brethren that were fent acrofs the
" Ganges ;" but *juftice, moderation,* and *good
faith,* have nothing to do with it.

" To quiet the fears of the Neighbouring
" Powers, who *from the conduct of our fer-
" vants* have had too much reafon to be
" jealous of our encroachments," and particularly to fettle a more mutually advantageous and fatisfactory alliance between the
Company and the Nabob Vizier of Oude,
was the grand motive which induced the
Governor General to proceed up the country. He found the Vizier much diftreffed
and much diffatisfied : his Government re-
laxed, his Finances greatly difordered, and
his Country in confufion. To augment, if
poffible, the produce of the Revenues, to
give vigour to the Executive Powers, and
tranquillity to the Kingdom, without alarming the Vizier's jealoufy towards any thing
that might feem to trench upon his independence,

pendence, and at the same time without prejudicing the interests of the Company, or committing their honour, required superior talents, the coolest discretion, and the most rigorous impartiality. Among the political evils to which it was found necessary to apply a remedy, the state of Lands granted in Jagheer seems to have been of the first importance. A profusion in the original donations, fraudulent mis-statements of their value, and abuses in the management of delegated jurisdiction, had left the Vizier but little unalienated property, and as little personal authority. The second article of the new treaty, in prescribing a palliative for these disorders, effectually establishes their existence. This article (not quoted in the Report) is as follows :

" That as great distress has arisen to the " Vizier's Government from the military " power and dominion assumed by the Jag- " heerdars, he be permitted to resume such " as he may find necessary, with a reserve " that all such *for the amount of whose Jag-* " *heers the Company are Guarantees,* shall, in " case of the resumption of their Lands, " be paid the amount of their nett collec- " tions, through the Resident, in ready mo- " ney."

Then immediately follows the *third Ar-*

N   *ticle;*

ticle, relative to Fyzoolah Khan, on which the Eighth Report is to ferve as a Comment.

"That as Fyzoolah Khan has by his "breach of Treaty forfeited the protection "of the Englifh Government, and caufes, "by his continuance in his prefent inde- "pendent State, great alarm and detriment "to the Nabob, he be permitted, when "time fhall fuit, to refume his lands, and "*pay him in Money,* through the Refident, "the *Amount ftipulated by Treaty,* after "deducting the amount and charges of the "Troops he ftands engaged to furnifh by "Treaty, which amount fhall be paffed to "the Account of the Company, during "the Continuance of the prefent War."

Other Jagheerdars, therefore, againft whom we hear of no explicit charge whatever, are to fuffer a refumption of their Lands; and why not Fyzoolah Khan? Many of *them,* we fee, are guaranteed by the Company as well as *he,* and a violation of the agreement on *his* part ftands upon record; *a flat refufal to execute what the Vizier had directed,* and a declaration "*that* "*he would abide by it.*" (Page 16.) If the Refumption of Jagheers in general were found a meafure connected with the fafety or welfare of the ftate, I fhould fuppofe

political

political neceffity a full juftification for its admiffion. But though the plea were allowed as far as concerned the other Jagheerdars, the Governor General's good fortune, combined with his prudence, interpofed to make the cafe of Fyzoolah Khan a fubject for a diftinct article. It indicates a thorough forefight of the malevolence of his enemies, that he fhould have provided for an attack on the feparate cafe of Fyzoolah Khan, which, to every perfon on the fpot, muft have appeared to be entirely blended with the general concerns of all the other Jagheerdars. But there is a nicety of conduct in this tranfaction, a delicacy of difcrimination between the actual rights or powers of the Vizier, and the policy of permitting their full exertion, that, while it cannot difprove the fact of Fyzoolah's forfeiture, is content to palliate its enormity ; and while the Governor General might juftly have reprobated the *open violation* of the treaty in the ftrongeft terms, he is fo moderate as to fay, in his Remarks on this third Article, " The conduct of Fyzoolah Khan, in " refufing the aid demanded, though *not an* " *abfolute breach* of the treaty, was *evafive* " and *uncandid.*" (Page 17.)

The fact is, that, had Mr. Haftings admitted to its fulleft extent, the whole cir-

cumftance

cumftance of the manifeft breach of the treaty, it would hardly have been warrantable in him to fcreen the Rohilla Chief, as he has done, from the utmoft effects of the Vizier's offended authority. But he knew, probably, as well as the Court of Directors, " *Fyzoolah Khan's merits with the* " *Company;*" he ftill recollected the former " *mark of his faithful attachment,*" in fending, " without hefitation or delay, 500 men " to co-operate with our forces ;" and being befides " of opinion that neither the " Vizier's nor the Company's interefts " would be promoted by depriving Fyzoo- " lah Khan of his independency," (page 17,) he fufpended the Vizier's claim, which he could not in point of equity attempt to controvert, and " *referved the execution of* " *the agreement to an indefinite term.*" Nothing, indeed, can, in my mind, exculpate the Governor General for fuch apparent interference and partial protection to the difobedient Subject of an independent Prince, " *which muft be known to all the fur-* " *rounding powers,*" and which may well excite " *future combinations againft us*" in thofe who from this example can but have " *too much reafon to be jealous of our en-* " *croachments*"—Nothing, I fay, can exculpate Mr. Haftings on this head, but the full-

nefs

nefs of his conviction, that it was neceffary for our Government to interpofe to prevent any ill effects from the violence of the Vizier's difpleafure, and the chance of dangerous commotions in the country.

On the whole, It is as clear as the fun, that Fyzoolah Khan was a fubject of the Vizier: that he had obtained, by an unfair valuation, Lands far beyond the amount of his Grant: that he had, by a direct breach of the Conditions on which thofe lands were held, forfeited all claim to the Company's Guarantee: that the Vizier had an inherent indifputable title to the refumption of the Jagheer: and that the Governor General, entirely from prudential motives, fufpended the Execution of that Juftice, and the Exertion of that Prerogative, to which he could but admit the folidity of the Vizier's pretenfions.

DETECTOR.

2 1ft *May*, 1783.

www.ingramcontent.com/pod-product-compliance
Lightning Source LLC
Chambersburg PA
CBHW032247080426
42735CB00008B/1043